My Velvet Elvis

*a memoir
of amazing animals*

My Velvet Elvis

*a memoir
of amazing animals*

Ruth L Kirk

MY VELVET ELVIS
Text and Photos Copyrighted by Ruth L Kirk 2019-2021
Published by Shamrock Press
P.O. BOX 58186
CHARLESTON WV 25358
USA
www.shamrockpress.com

Cover design and typesetting: Sandy Tritt and Eric Fritzius

Printed and bound in America.
ALL RIGHTS RESERVED.
No part of this publication may be reproduced, stored in a retrieval system, or transmitted in any form or by any means, electronic, mechanical, photocopying, recording, or otherwise, without the prior written permission of the publisher. This includes REPLACING THE BOOK COVER in any form for resale.

Library of Congress Control Number: 2018913120
ISBN 0-9675410-6-9
ISBN 978-0-9675410-6-8

SECOND EDITION NOVEMBER 2021

PRINTED IN THE UNITED STATES OF AMERICA

I rescued him . . .
and THEN he rescued me.

AND SO IT WAS…

My daughter and I arrived at the animal shelter to see a dog up for adoption named Wolfgang Puck, which I thought was an adorable name. He was a cute, mixed-breed Jack Russell terrier.

The shelter wasn't open yet, so we found a place to eat lunch. I wasn't sure I was ready for another dog at this time in my life. In fact, I purposely did not even bring a collar, lead or carrier in which to take a dog home. I just wanted to look—and look only. Commitment might come later, if at all. I had lost my Shih Tzu a year earlier, and, more recently, a one-of-a-kind German shepherd named All That Jazz. We loved Jazz, and when she died, my husband said no more dogs—especially not another German shepherd—as none could equal our Jazz. He was right about that. We'd had German shepherds in our lives for over fifty years, and we loved each and every one of them. But Jazz was special.

We returned to the shelter to find Wolfgang was out for a walk with one of the volunteers. My daughter suggested we look in the puppy room.

As we entered, the dog in the first cage was frantic, barking excessively, dumping his food and water, and tearing up the newspaper in the bottom of his cage. "I know I don't want that dog," I said. So we checked out the other pups, which were being rapidly claimed.

Next we went to see the older dogs. Most were very large—and very active—and too much for me to handle. So we continue our search for the right dog.

We then went to the cat room. We love cats, too.

Finally, we were told Wolfgang was back, and we went out to see him. We took him for a walk. He was only interested in himself and not us, and I did not feel a connection to him. If one is going to have a pet for many years, it's essential the chemistry is right.

My daughter suggested we go back into the puppy room one more time.

Well, that noisy and destructive dog was still there. My daughter asked the attendant if she would let him out. When the cage opened, the dog ran to my daughter like she were a long-lost friend. I knew he had won her over. Not so much me, though.

My daughter suggested we take him over to the cat room to see his reaction to cats, being as two cats live at our home.

So we did. He loved all the cats and wagged his tail at them. They did not all like him, but he didn't seem to care. In the corner of the room was a glassed-in run with a mother pit bull and her pups. He trotted over to make friends. If that glass partition hadn't been there, he would've been a goner.

But he wagged his tail and tried to be friendly regardless. *Wow.*

My daughter decided we would adopt him. I went along with it, although I still had my doubts. It was Adopt a Hound Dog Week in celebration of Elvis's birthday, and since Elvis was one of my favorite singers, we named him Elvis. His black fur was like velvet, so I called him my Velvet Elvis.

He rode home with my daughter that day, sitting on her lap and helping to drive the car. He has been in the driver's seat at our home ever since.

Not having had a dog for over a year, I wasn't exactly prepared. I had given away the dog bowls, food, leashes, collars, and beds.

So I improvised, using our bowls and food like Tom's excellent spaghetti. That suited Elvis.

I was ready for bed on our first snowy night together when Elvis decided he had to go out. I was sporting my new bedroom slippers, so I took him out on the front porch with plans to stay on the porch while he did his thing.

Well, he jumped off the porch, into a snow drift, and disappeared. *Good grief!* I thought.

Our last dog had been a tall German shepherd, but Elvis was short. Maybe he was lost in the snow drift. I hurried to get my boots, worried he might suffocate.

As I turned to go into the house, Elvis literally jumped out of the snow, then joyously dived into another pile. This was his kind of weather.

I finally brought him in and dried him off.

Elvis started out sleeping in a large crate in the utility room, since we didn't know if he was potty trained. Then he moved into the living room. Then, lo and behold, he moved into our bedroom—and then on our bed.

In fifty years of married life, we had never let a dog or cat sleep on our bed.

I'm not really sure how Elvis managed it, but Elvis has charming ways.

Months passed, and I was having difficulty walking and had pain in my right side. This went on for almost two years. My health deteriorated, and when I got up at night to use the bathroom, Elvis got up with me. He would sit right next to me and look at me with the kindest eyes. He never left my side, whatever I was doing.

At that same time, my husband was having heart problems, and Elvis would sit on his lap, offering comfort to him. Elvis had a calming effect on both of us.

Eventually, I had an operation to remove a tumor from my spine, and was in the hospital for two weeks and two days. Elvis was a lot of company for my husband during this time. My daughter-in-law put Elvis's picture on my iPhone. I looked at it many times during my stay at the hospital. It was another reason to get home.

When I came home, Elvis was beyond excited. He attached himself to me and refused to leave my side. He made sure the home health people took good care of me. He inspected them and their black bags—perhaps checking for treats?

They, in turn, always greeted him, and some *did* bring him treats.

As the nurse took my vitals, Elvis would stare at her, focused on what she was doing. He had a way of staring right into the eyes of the caregivers, letting them know he was in charge. Most of them could not help but laugh out loud. Elvis became the subject of their weekly meetings, I was told. Elvis stories reigned.

One day the physical therapist was working with me on balance. I stood at the kitchen sink to do my exercises. In order to get a better view, Elvis jumped onto a kitchen chair to watch. On this particular day, though, he fell off the chair.

He was okay, just a little shook up. We all laughed out loud, and I told him he needed to work on his balance.

Elvis has a habit of taking one of my shoes and one of my husband's, and putting them on his rug. You'd have to ask Elvis why he does this, but I suspect it's his way of keeping track of us.

Elvis was a big part of my healing process, and, along with my family, of course, a good reason to get well.

My Velvet Elvis turned out to be a special gift from God. Thank you, Lord.

TANNY

HE LOVED ME . . .

He seemed to be a figment of my imagination. I caught a glimpse of him out of the corner of my eye when I stepped out on my back deck, but then he was gone.

This continued off and on for weeks.

And then one day I caught full sight of him. He was a handsome, tan and white collie. He looked like a smaller version of Lassie, the movie star dog. He was definitely a mixed breed, but part of his tan coat had a gleaming reddish shine that made him especially handsome.

Since it seemed he was after the cat food I put out on the deck for our cats, I started putting food out for him.

It took an entire whole year before he would let me get near enough to pet him. He was so shy and afraid, I was certain he'd been mistreated. Gaining his trust wasn't easy, but eventually, I did. Not entirely, though, as he always had that little doubt that maybe I'd hurt him, so I had to be careful in handling him. Yet, he turned out to be a faithful and true friend.

He followed me everywhere, but at a safe distance. When I went out to feed the horses, he came with me.

Later, when I owned the boarding kennel, he followed me on my rounds there.

Since I required the dogs who boarded at the kennel to have all their shots, I knew I'd have to somehow corral Tanny so the vet could give him his shots.

Well, that was an adventure too. Perhaps, I might add, a dangerous and risky adventure.

Tanny had appointed himself my guardian, which was both good and bad.

The day came for the veterinarian to come out for a farm call. With so many animals—horses, dogs, and cats—the vet would come to us.

Catching Tanny off guard was not easy. Since he had the habit of following me everywhere, I let him follow me into one of our outside dog runs, which was eight-feet long. I hurried out of the run and shut him in. Good, so far.

Later, when the vet arrived, I explained the problem with this frightened dog who had probably never had any shots. I told him my plan. I would slip a looped leash over his head and pass it through the wire fence in the adjoining kennel run.

I would then tighten it securely and hang on to Tanny with all my strength so the Vet could step in and give him his shots.

I held him very tightly against the wire from the other side of the adjoining dog run.

The Vet had the shots ready, and quickly gave them to a nervous and angry dog.

Mission accomplished.

Or so we thought.

I turned Tanny lose, figuring he would hightail it out of the kennel run and head for open fields.

At least, that was the plan.

Well, Tanny did hightail it. He ran for all he was worth. We had left the walkway free and the doors and gates open so he could make his escape. And off he went.

The vet and I both sighed a breath of relief—especially me.

Next, the vet stood up with needle in hand to vaccinate the next dog. He stood behind me with needle raised. The next thing I knew, Tanny was on the attack. He had run back from freedom, raced around me, and attacked the vet's leg.

My mouth flew open and I was wordless. So many thoughts flew through my mind—mainly that I was probably going to be bitten when I tried to pry open Tanny's mouth to free the vet. But I had to do it. I told the vet that as soon as I was able to get Tanny off his leg, he should go into the cage and shut the gate behind him.

It took a while, but I finally got Tanny's teeth out of his leg.

The vet stepped into the cage and secured the gate. Good move.

I chased Tanny out of the kennel and shut the front gate and the gate leading to the walkway before I helped the vet out of the cage.

"At least Tanny has had his rabies shot," I said, and then apologized profusely.

This turn of events certainly caught me by surprise—and, of course, the vet too.

One snowy and very icy day, I walked out to the kennel to let the dogs out in their runs.

I was alone that day—the kids were in school and my husband was at work.

As I started down the walkway to the kennel gate, I slipped on the ice and fell backward, hitting my head. I could not move. It was freezing. I was freezing.

This predated cell phones, so I had no help.. Snow fell down on me. The cold of the ice bed below me quickly permeated my coat. What could I do? I'd freeze to death before anyone found me.

I tried to move my arm, but I couldn't.

TANNY ran to me and whined for me to get up.

"I can't move," I explained to him.

He pawed around me, looking for a way to get me up. There was nothing he could do. Finally, he lay across my chest. He was like a fur blanket covering my most important body parts.

As we lay there, snow continued to fall, covering him as well as me. But he would not leave me.

Eventually I was able to get up and all was well, but it was scary until Tanny came and was there for me. He didn't move until I asked him to. He kept me warm and safe. I will always be thankful for this wonderful dog who appeared out of know where and enriched my life.

BABE

I CRIED . . .

I cried while watching the movie *Flicka*. Flicka was a wild mustang loved by a girl, but not the girl's father. After many mishaps, Flicka finally won the hearts of all the family. Watching this movie brought back memories of my beloved horse, Babe.

When I was four, my mother died. The year she was so sick, I spent time in a neighbor's pasture watching the horses. One day, some boys chased the horses, swinging sticks at them. The horses ran helter-skelter in fear. I sprinted after the boys, dodging between the horses. "Get out!" I yelled. "I'm going to tell!"

Knowing what I know now, I don't know why I wasn't run over by the excited horses. They were running, actually galloping, their eyes large with fear and their nostrils flared. But they did not run over me. They seemed to understand I was there to help. That was when I realized that someday I'd have to have a horse of my own. I loved the creatures.

When I was in my early twenties, I paid all of five hundred dollars for Babe, my first horse, my dream come true. She was small, but I was short and could put my arm over her back, so she was perfect for me. At the time, I was a young housewife and mother blessed with a loving husband who indulged my love of horses.

My short horse grew into a larger horse. I could no longer reach my arm across her back. Tom, my husband, had to break her to accept the saddle and to ride, which he did. Neither of us really knew what we were doing, but it worked out okay. In hindsight, we must've had guardian angels looking over us.

It was costly to board Babe, so we started looking for a farm with a stable. Eventually, we bought a farm where we lived and raised our children, and it was on our farm that Babe and I grew close.

Like Flicka, Babe had a mind of her own. She knew what she wanted and she was determined to get it. I appreciated her independence, her spirit. Just being around Babe taught me a lot about horses—enough that I felt confident enough to take the next step.

To help pay for the farm, feed and grain, I started boarding horses. Not just any horses, but thoroughbred horses hot off the track. Although I thought I knew a lot about horses, I was wrong. Many times, Babe saved me from my inadequate knowledge. I would have been killed or a least badly injured if she had not been there to help me and protect me.

When I brought the horses in from the pasture and the thoroughbreds were about to run me down, Babe ran in front of them to slow them down. She was the queen, the empress, the ruler of the herd, and she made sure they knew it. She kept order. She always came when I called her, and the other horses would follow.

After an exhausting day, I would go up to the stable porch and stand by Babe's stall door and pet her soft nose. It brought comfort to me. Then Babe would lean out over her door and put her head on my shoulder. She would sigh as if agreeing with my unspoken thoughts. I would then sit on the bench for a while, just enjoying her company and hearing her snorts and sighs.

One day, while riding with friends into the forest, we were so busy talking that we got lost. Believe me, one tree looks like another when you're in a forest.

There were four of us, and each had a different opinion of which trail led to home. Finally, I decided to trust Babe. She undoubtedly knew the way home—and it was getting past time for her evening feeding, so I knew she was hungry. I turned her reins loose and told her to take us home. She did. In record time.

Over the years, our bond deepened. Tom and I were away one weekend, and when we returned home, my kennel and barn helpers informed me that Babe had colic. She had suffered from colic once before and survived. For non-horse people, colic is like a severe stomachache. Unfortunately, horses cannot throw up, or, in nicer language, *regurgitate*. The only thing left to do was to give the horse a gigantic dose of a laxative concoction in hopes the blockage would expel via nature's natural exit.

The veterinarian came to our farm and gave her the dose. The next step was to walk the horse until the medication had the desired effects. The horse cannot lie down, as this will cause his intestines to twist and kill the horse. So we walked. And walked.

Tom relieved me from time to time, but Babe was on her feet for almost three days. I was sick with worry. Would she recover? She was older, at least twenty- five years, but in good shape for her age. I had not ridden her in years, but I still enjoyed watching her out in the paddock and having her around the farm. Simply being with her was enough. We understood each other completely. She was my companion, my friend, my confidante.

It was on the third night that Tom and I took a break from walking Babe. We were downstairs in our office when Babe walked up to the office window and peered in. I jumped up. She had never done this before, and I knew she needed help.

I rushed outside. I rubbed her neck and looked into her eyes. She seemed glad I was with her, but what was she trying to tell me? That her condition had not improved, would not improve?

Tom appeared at my side. "We need to call the vet," he said quietly.

My stomach churned, but I knew he was right. He stayed with Babe while I ran in and called the veterinarian. I asked him to come out and check her one last time and tell us if it was time. I was told that no one was available for farm calls, but we could come to the office and get a shot to have on hand to put Babe down, if it became necessary. I was heartbroken and angry. I wanted the veterinarian, the expert, to help make the decision if we should put Babe down.

These same vets had taken care of her for twenty-five years, and now, when I needed them most, they couldn't be bothered to come out.

Even though we were well aware that only a veterinarian should put down a horse, Tom went and got the shot to have on hand so Babe wouldn't suffer needlessly.

When he returned, Tom and I walked Babe together. He led her to a spot in our pasture under an old oak tree where she liked to stand on sunny hot days.

"If we have to put her down, let's do it here," he said. "It will be a good place to bury her, and we won't have to move her." Babe weighed around eleven hundred pounds, so she would not be easy to move.

I sighed. "With all my heart, I hope we don't have to do that." I closed my eyes, a shiver running down my spine. "I just don't think I have it in me to give her that injection. For the rest of my life, I'd wonder if it was the right thing to do." I turned to Babe. "Come on, Babe. Let's walk. Let's keep trying."

The night wore on. The weather was warm enough but not too hot, and a cool breeze filtered the air. The country sky was bright with stars. I needed to use the restroom, so I brought Babe with me to the front yard. "I'll be right back," I assured her, then ran into the house. I hurried, but when I returned to the yard, Babe was gone.

She couldn't have gone far, so I headed toward the pasture. And that's when I saw her. She was lying on her side, in the pasture, under the old oak tree, exactly where Tom had wanted her to be. I ran to her and dropped down on my knees next to her. She was gone.

And, so like Babe, she went on her own terms—but, also so like Babe, with me on her mind. She had listened to the conversation Tom and I had about the best place for her to die, about how I didn't want to have to use the injection. Despite her pain and exhaustion, she made sure she spared us.

I cried.

The End

Author's Note

BABE IS A TRUE STORY. Needless to say, I was devastated at Babe's passing, but I'm thankful the veterinarian did what he thought was in the best interest of the horse so she would not suffer needlessly.

www.ingramcontent.com/pod-product-compliance
Lightning Source LLC
Chambersburg PA
CBHW071646040426
42452CB00009B/1782